Funny Quotes
Serious People

Daily quotes for a better day

brain-words.com

About

This book does not intend to be a source of truth or bibliographical reference but a collection of funny and clever quotes.

The quotes in this book were collected from different sources and time periods. And a lot of effort has been made to quote the original author.

When sharing the quotes with other people please use the right author as identified in each quote.

services of a competent professional person should be sought. Neither the publisher nor the author shall be liable for damages arising herefrom. The fact that an individual, organization or website is referred to in this work as a citation and/or potential source of further information does not mean that the author or the publisher endorses the information the individual, organization or website may provide or recommendations they/it may make. Further, readers should be aware that Internet websites listed in this work may have changed or disappeared between when this work was written and when it is read. For general information on our other products and services or to obtain technical support, please contact us.

ISBN: 9781073821877

For more information visit:

www.brain-words.com

Contents

Introduction

What do Albert Einstein, Winston Churchill, and Abraham Lincoln have in common?

They were great achievers, and had a great sense of humor!

This book is a collection of the 365 funniest and cleverest quotes from remarkable people across history. They were artists, inventors, business people, politicians; and despite their busy lives, they had always time for a good laugh.

I believe we should do the same. We should take a break, laugh, and have a better life. That's what this book is about.

Have a happy day!

— brain-words.com

How to get the most out of this book

What I know from life is that laugh and funny stories give us pleasure and can be powerful to combat stress and conflict; it helps to strengthen relationships and make new ones.

People with a good sense of humor that can tell a good story or joke live better, have more opportunities and are less affected by the daily routine.

You can use this book as you please but here are a few ways that I have thought:

• Read one quote per day: Make it a daily routine, this will bring pieces of happiness each day during the year

• Share with your friends: As Einstein said: "The best way to cheer yourself is to cheer somebody else up."; share the quotes with your friend, at work, start a meeting with a funny quote to break the ice.

• Read the book from cover to cover like any other book.

Funny Story 1:

Albert Einstein's wife often suggested that he dress more professionally,

when he headed off to work.

"Why should I?" he would invariably argue.

Everyone knows me there."

When the time came for Einstein to attend his first major conference,

she begged him to dress up a bit.

"Why should I?" said Einstein.

"No one knows me there

January

January 1

"When you are courting a nice girl an hour seems like a second. When you sit on a red-hot cinder a second seems like an hour. That's relativity."

— Albert Einstein

January 2

"Never put off till tomorrow what you can do the day after tomorrow."

— Mark Twain

January 3

"You and I come by road or rail, but economists travel on infrastructure."

— Margaret Thatcher

January 4

"I'd like to live like a poor man—only with lots of money."

— Pablo Picasso

January 5

"In this world, nothing can be said to be certain, except death and taxes."

— Benjamin Franklin

January 6

"I always arrive late at the office, but I make up for it by leaving early."

— Charles Lamb

January 7

"I may be drunk, Miss, but in the morning I will be sober and you will still be ugly."

— Winston Churchill

January 8

"Politicians are a lot like diapers. They should be changed frequently, and for the same reasons."

— Benjamin Franklin

January 9

"A girl should be two things: classy and fabulous."

— Coco Chanel

January 10

"Any customer can have a car painted any color that he wants so long as it is black."

— Henry Ford

January 11

"The world is a stage and the play is badly cast."

— Oscar Wilde

January 12

"Behind every successful man is a woman, behind her is his wife."

— Groucho Marx

January 13

"Good advice is something a man gives when he is too old to set a bad example."

— Francois de La Rochefoucauld

January 14

"Times are bad. Children no longer obey their parents, and everyone is writing a book."

— Cicero. M Tullius

January 15

"People who think they know everything are a great annoyance to those of us who do."

— Isaac Asimov

January 16

"I once spent a year in Philadelphia, I think it was on a Sunday."

W. C. Fields

January 17

"No dumb bastard ever won a war by going out and dying for his country. He won it by making some other dumb bastard die for his country."

— George S. Patton Jr.

January 18

"There is nothing in the world so irresistibly contagious as laughter and good humor."

— Charles Dickens, A Christmas Carol

January 19

"All you need in this life is ignorance and confidence; then success is sure. "

— Mark Twain

January 20

"If there's life on other planets, then the earth is the Universe's insane asylum."

— Voltaire

January 21

"It's hard to lead a cavalry charge if you think you look funny on a horse."

— Adlai E. Stevenson

January 22

"Creativity is knowing how to hide your sources"

— C.E.M. Joad

January 23

"Cultivate your curves - they may be dangerous but they won't be avoided."

— Mae West

January 24

"Personally, I'm always ready to learn, although I do not always like being taught."

— Winston S. Churchill

January 25

"A man doesn't know what he knows until he knows what he doesn't know."

— Laurence J. Peter

January 26

"Three be the things I shall never attain: Envy, content, and sufficient champagne."

— Dorothy Parker

January 27

"The world is full of magical things patiently waiting for our wits to grow sharper."

— Bertrand Russell

January 28

"If you're going to tell people the truth, be funny or they'll kill you."

— Billy Wilder

January 29

"All right everyone, line up alphabetically according to your height."

— Casey Stengel

January 30

"Animals are my friends...and I don't eat my friends."

— George Bernard Shaw

January 31

"Everything in the world is about sex except sex. Sex is about power."

— Oscar Wilde

February

February 1

"Once I had a rose named after me and I was very flattered. But I was not pleased to read the description in the catalog: "No good in a bed, but fine up against a wall."

— Eleanor Roosevelt

February 2

"I've got all the money I'll ever need; if I die by four o'clock."

— Henny Youngman

February 3

"The best argument against democracy is a five-minute conversation with the average voter."

— Winston S. Churchill

February 4

"When I was a boy of 14, my father was so ignorant I could hardly stand to have the old man around. But when I got to be 21, I was astonished at how much the old man had learned in seven years."

— Mark Twain

February 5

"If there are no dogs in Heaven, then when I die I want to go where they went."

— Will Rogers

February 6

"There are two theories to arguing with a woman. Neither works."

— Will Rogers

February 7

"You only live once, but if you do it right, once is enough."

— Mae West

February 8

"Never interrupt your enemy when he is making a mistake."

— Napoleon Bonaparte

February 9

"A man in love is incomplete until he has married. Then he's finished."

— Zsa Zsa Gabor

February 10

"He that displays too often his wife and his wallet is in danger of having both of them borrowed."

— Benjamin Franklin

February 11

"You cannot be anything if you want to be everything."

— Solomon Schechter

February 12

"If you're going through hell, keep going."

— Winston Churchill

February 13

It is so pleasant to come across people more stupid than ourselves. We love them at once for being so.

— Jerome K. Jerome

February 14

"Never miss a good chance to shut up."

— Will Rogers

February 15

"But I am thinking like a lover, or like an ass: which I suppose is pretty nearly the same."

– Charles Dickens

February 16

"People often say that motivation doesn't last. Well, neither does bathing – that's why we recommend it daily."

– Zig Ziglar

February 17

"The short memories of the American voters is what keeps our politicians in office."

– Will Rogers

February 18

"Man has his will, but woman has her way."

– Oliver Wendell Holmes Sr.

February 19

"Men marry women with the hope they will never change. Women marry men with the hope they will change. Invariably they are both disappointed."

– Albert Einstein

February 20

"Learn from the mistakes of others. You can never live long enough to make them all yourself."

— Groucho Marx

February 21

"Roses are red, violets are blue, I'm schizophrenic, and so am I."

— Oscar Levant

February 22

"All I know is just what I read in the papers, and that's an alibi for my ignorance."

— Will Rogers

February 23

"Marry, and you will regret it; don't marry, you will also regret it; marry or don't marry, you will regret it either way."

— Søren Kierkegaard

February 24

"Don't interrupt me while I'm interrupting."

— Winston S. Churchill

February 25

"The best thing about the future is that it comes one day at a time."

– Abraham Lincoln

February 26

"Those are my principles, and if you don't like them...well I have others."

– Groucho Marx

February 27

"History will be kind to me for I intend to write it."

– Winston S. Churchill

February 28

"I have never made but one prayer to God, a very short one: Oh Lord, make my enemies ridiculous. And God granted it."

– Voltaire

February 29

"The comfort of the rich depends upon an abundant supply of the poor."

– Voltaire

March

March 1

"We learn from experience that men never learn anything from experience."

– George Bernard Shaw

March 2

"I must have a prodigious amount of mind; it takes me as much as a week, sometimes, to make it up!"

– Mark Twain

March 3

"Do not take life too seriously. You will never get out of it alive."

– Elbert Hubbard

March 4

"Life is hard. After all, it kills you."

– Katharine Hepburn

March 5

"Education is learning what you didn't even know you didn't know."

– Daniel J. Boorstin

March 6

"Never memorize something that you can look up."

– Albert Einstein

March 7

"Trouble knocked at the door, but, hearing laughter, hurried away."

– Benjamin Franklin

March 8

"High heels were invented by a woman who had been kissed on the forehead."

– Christopher Morley

March 9

"If at first you don't succeed, try, try again. Then quit. No use being a damn fool about it."

– W.C. Fields

March 10

"It's just a job. Grass grows, birds fly, waves pound the sand. I beat people up."

– Muhammad Ali

March 11

"My wife Mary and I have been married for forty-seven years and not once have we had an argument serious enough to consider divorce; murder, yes, but divorce, never."

– Jack Benny

March 12

"My pessimism extends to the point of even suspecting the sincerity of other pessimists."

– Jean Rostand

March 13

"Americans are incredibly impatient. Someone once said that the shortest period of time in America is the time between when the light turns green and when you hear the first horn honk."

– Jim Rohn

March 14

"A day without laughter is a day wasted."

— Charlie Chaplin

March 15

"A man's true character comes out when he's drunk."

— Charlie Chaplin

March 16

"Quotation, n: The act of repeating erroneously the words of another."

— Ambrose Bierce, The Unabridged Devil's Dictionary

March 17

"If you don't get everything you want, think of the things you don't get that you don't want."

— Oscar Wilde

March 18

"A pessimist is somebody who complains about the noise when opportunity knocks."

— Oscar Wilde

March 19

"I came from a real tough neighborhood. Why, every time I shut the window I hurt somebody's fingers."

— Rodney Dangerfield

March 20

"Half our life is spent trying to find something to do with the time we have rushed through life trying to save."

– Will Rogers

March 21

"I once had a rose named after me and I was very flattered. But I was not pleased to read the description in the catalogue: no good in a bed, but fine up against a wall."

– Eleanor Roosevelt

March 22

"Life begins at 40 – but so do fallen arches, rheumatism, faulty eyesight, and the tendency to tell a story to the same person, three or four times."

– Helen Rowland

March 23

"A photographer is like a cod, which produces a million eggs in order that one may reach maturity."

– George Bernard Shaw

March 24

"Two wrongs don't make a right, but they make a good excuse."

— Thomas Szasz

March 25

"If you're too open-minded; your brains will fall out."

— Lawrence Ferlinghetti

March 26

"It's a recession when your neighbor loses his job; it's a depression when you lose your own."

— Harry S. Truman

March 27

"God did not intend religion to be an exercise club."

— Naguib Mahfouz

March 28

"A woman's mind is cleaner than a man's: She changes it more often."

— Oliver Herford

March 29

"A successful man is one who makes more money than his wife can spend. A successful woman is one who can find such a man."

– Lana Turner

March 30

"A stockbroker urged me to buy a stock that would triple its value every year. I told him, 'At my age, I don't even buy green bananas.'"

– Claude Pepper

March 31

"An old battleax of a woman said to Winston Churchill, "If you were my husband I would put poison in your tea." Churchill's response, "Ma'am if you were my wife I would drink it."

– Winston S. Churchill

Funny Story 2

Abraham Lincoln told a story of a time he was splitting rails when a man carrying a rifle walked up to him and demanded that Lincoln look him directly in the eye.

Lincoln stopped his work and obliged the man, who continued to silently stare at him for some minutes.

Finally, the man told Lincoln that he "had promised himself years ago that if he ever met a man uglier than himself, he would shoot him."

Lincoln looked at the man's rifle mischievously and said nothing.

Finally, Lincoln pulled open his shirt, threw out his chest, and exclaimed, "If I am uglier than you, go ahead and shoot; because I don't want to live!"

April

April 1

"There are always some lunatics about. It would be a dull world without them."

— Sir Arthur Conan Doyle, The Red Headed League

April 2

"Thinking is the hardest work there is, which is probably the reason so few engage in it."

— Henry Ford

April 3

"Here's to our wives and girlfriends...may they never meet!"

— Groucho Marx

April 4

"Imagination was given to man to compensate him for what he is not; a sense of humor to console him for what he is."

— Francis Bacon

April 5

"When I was a boy I was told that anybody could become President. I'm beginning to believe it."

– Clarence Darrow

April 6

"Marriage is the only war in which you sleep with the enemy."

– Francois de La Rochefoucauld

April 7

"A joke is a very serious thing."

– Winston S. Churchill

April 8

"It would be nice to spend billions on schools and roads, but right now that money is desperately needed for political ads."

– Andy Borowitz

April 9

"When I hear somebody sigh, 'Life is hard,' I am always tempted to ask, 'Compared to what?'"

– Sydney J. Harris

April 10

"Forgive, O Lord, my little jokes on Thee. And I'll forgive Thy great big one on me."

— Robert Frost

April 11

"Men are all the same, they think that because they came out of the belly of a woman they know all there is to know about women."

— José Saramago

April 12

"To those of you who received honours, awards and distinctions, I say well done. And to the C students, I say you, too, can be president of the United States."

— George W. Bush

April 13

"I find television very educating. Every time somebody turns on the set, I go into the other room and read a book."

— Groucho Marx

April 14

"Common sense is the most widely shared commodity in the world, for every man is convinced that he is well supplied with it."

— Rene Descartes

April 15

"If you can't explain it to a six year old, you don't understand it yourself."

— Albert Einstein

April 16

"Better to remain silent and be thought a fool than to speak out and remove all doubt."

— Abraham Lincoln

April 17

"At every party there are two kinds of people – those who want to go home and those who don't. The trouble is, they are usually married to each other."

— Ann Landers

April 18

"He who can do—he who cannot, teaches."

George Bernard Shaw

April 19

"Doctors are just the same as lawyers; the only difference is that lawyers merely rob you, whereas doctors rob you and kill you too."

– Anton Chekhov

April 20

"Always go to other people's funerals, otherwise they won't come to yours."

– Yogi Berra

April 21

"Be who you are and say what you feel, because those who mind don't matter and those who matter don't mind."

– Bernard Baruch

April 22

"I'd rather have 1% of the effort of 100 men than 100% of my own effort."

– J. Paul Getty

April 23

"I don't think anyone should write their autobiography until after they're dead."

– Samuel Goldwyn

April 24

"Analyzing humor is like dissecting a frog. Few people are interested and the frog dies of it."

— E. B. White

April 25

"The most important decision you make is to be in a good mood."

— Voltaire

April 26

"I never travel without my diary. One should always have something sensational to read in the train."

— Oscar Wilde, The Importance of Being Earnest

April 27

"Wine is constant proof that God loves us and loves to see us happy."

— Benjamin Franklin

April 28

"It takes a lot of time to be a genius. You have to sit around so much, doing nothing, really doing nothing."

— Gertrude Stein

April 29

"It's a shame that the only thing a man can do for eight hours a day is work. He can't eat for eight hours; he can't drink for eight hours; he can't make love for eight hours. The only thing a man can do for eight hours is work. "

— William Faulkner

April 30

"We are all here on earth to help others; what on earth the others are here for I don't know."

— W. H. Auden

May

May 1

"Age is an issue of mind over matter. If you don't mind, it doesn't matter."

– Mark Twain

May 2

"Nobody realizes that some people expend tremendous energy merely to be normal."

– Albert Camus

May 3

"Everything not forbidden is compulsory"

– T.H. White, The Once and Future King

May 4

"I can stand brute force, but brute reason is quite unbearable. There is something unfair about its use. It is hitting below the intellect."

– Oscar Wilde

May 5

"Originality is the fine art of remembering what you hear but forgetting where you heard it."

– Laurence J. Peter

May 6

"Everybody laughs the same in every language because laughter is a universal connection."

– Yakov Smirnoff

May 7

"Always carry a flagon of whiskey in case of snakebite and furthermore always carry a small snake."

– W. C. Fields

May 8

"When we remember we are all mad, the mysteries disappear and life stands explained."

– Mark Twain

May 9

"I don't want to go to heaven. None of my friends are there."

– Oscar Wilde

May 10

"I did not attend his funeral, but I sent a nice letter saying I approved of it."

— Mark Twain

May 11

"I have not failed. I've just found 10,000 ways that won't work."

— Thomas A. Edison

May 12

"Always forgive your enemies; nothing annoys them so much."

— Oscar Wilde

May 13

"I cook with wine, sometimes I even add it to the food."

— W.C. Fields

May 14

"A committee is a group that keeps minutes and loses hours."

— Milton Berle

May 15

"The cure for boredom is curiosity. There is no cure for curiosity."

– Dorothy Parker

May 16

"Be careful about reading health books. You may die of a misprint."

– Mark Twain

May 17

"I wrote the story myself. It's about a girl who lost her reputation and never missed it."

– Mae West

May 18

"When I die, I want to die like my grandfather who died peacefully in his sleep. Not screaming like all the passengers in his car."

– Will Rogers

May 19

"It is better to be alone than in bad company."

– George Washington

May 20

"I have tried to know absolutely nothing about a great many things, and I have succeeded fairly well."

– Robert Benchley

May 21

"By working faithfully eight hours a day you may eventually get to be boss and work twelve hours a day."

– Robert Frost

May 22

"Love is an irresistible desire to be irresistibly desired."

– Robert Frost

May 23

"I hate mankind, for I think myself one of the best of them, and I know how bad I am."

– Samuel Johnson

May 24

"If you must make a noise, make it quietly."

– Oliver Hardy

May 25

"The chief function of the body is to carry the brain around."

— Thomas A. Edison

May 26

"Between two evils, I always pick the one I never tried before."

— Mae West

May 27

"Go to Heaven for the climate, Hell for the company."

— Mark Twain

May 28

"Light travels faster than sound. This is why some people appear bright until you hear them speak."

– Alan Dundes

May 29

"This life's hard, but it's harder if you're stupid."

— George V. Higgins, The Friends of Eddie Coyle

May 30

"Perhaps it is better to be irresponsible and right, than to be responsible and wrong."

— Winston S. Churchill

May 31

"I am dying by inches, from not having anybody to talk to about insects."

— Charles Darwin

June

June 1

"Mirrors should think longer before they reflect."

— Jean Cocteau

June 2

"I am so clever that sometimes I don't understand a single word of what I am saying."

— Oscar Wilde, The Happy Prince and Other Stories

June 3

"If pro is the opposite of con, what is the opposite of Congress?"

— Will Rogers

June 4

"I have the simplest tastes. I am always satisfied with the best."

— Oscar Wilde

June 5

"In politics, stupidity is not a handicap."

— Napoleon Bonaparte

June 6

"If you could kick the person in the pants responsible for most of your trouble, you wouldn't sit for a month."

— Theodore Roosevelt

June 7

"I'm not the smartest fellow in the world, but I can sure pick smart colleagues."

— Franklin D. Roosevelt

June 8

"We hang the petty thieves and appoint the great ones to public office."

— Aesop

June 9

It is always the best policy to speak the truth, unless, of course, you are an exceptionally good liar.

— Jerome K. Jerome

June 10

"If I had asked people what they wanted, they would have said faster horses."

— Henry Ford

June 11

"The duty of a patriot is to protect his country from its government."

– Edward Abbey

June 12

"My mother said to me, 'If you are a soldier, you will become a general. If you are a monk, you will become the Pope.' Instead, I was a painter, and became Picasso."

– Pablo Picasso

June 13

"If you think you are too small to make a difference, try sleeping with a mosquito."

– Dalai Lama

June 14

"Never have more children than you have car windows."

– Erma Bombeck

June 15

"My tastes are simple: I am easily satisfied with the best."

– Winston S. Churchill

June 16

 "Knowledge is knowing a tomato is a fruit; wisdom is not putting it in a fruit salad."

– Miles Kington

June 17

"Don't be so humble - you are not that great."

– Golda Meir

June 18

"I've lived through some terrible things in my life, some of which actually happened."

– Mark Twain

June 19

"If you want your children to listen, try talking softly to someone else."

– Ann Landers

June 20

"It is harder to crack prejudice than an atom."

– Albert Einstein

June 21

"Get your facts first, then you can distort them as you please."

— Mark Twain

June 22

"All are lunatics, but he who can analyze his delusion is called a philosopher."

— Ambrose Bierce,

June 23

"Never put off till tomorrow what may be done day after tomorrow just as well."

— Mark Twain

June 24

"The only mystery in life is why the kamikaze pilots wore helmets."

— Al McGuire

June 25

"I can resist everything except temptation."

— Oscar Wilde

June 26

"It is by the goodness of God that in our country we have those 3 unspeakably precious things: freedom of speech, freedom of conscience, and the prudence never to practice either of them."

— Mark Twain

June 29

"Give me a woman who loves beer and I will conquer the world."

— Wilhelm II

June 30

"Life is hard; it's harder if you're stupid."

— John Wayne

Funny Story 3

Abraham Lincolntold of the preacher that said, during his sermon, that although the Lord was the only perfect man, the Bible never mentioned a perfect woman.

A woman in the rear of the congregation called out:

"I know a perfect woman, and I've heard of her every day for the last six years."

"Who was she?" asked the surprised minister.

"My husband's first wife," came the reply.

July

July 1

"Never wrestle with pigs. You both get dirty and the pig likes it."

— George Bernard Shaw

July 2

"The road to success is dotted with many tempting parking spaces."

— Will Rogers

July 3

"There are two motives for reading a book; one, that you enjoy it; the other, that you can boast about it."

— Bertrand Russell

July 4

"Everyone is ignorant, only on different subjects."

— Will Rogers

July 5

"Ask me no questions, and I'll tell you no lies."

— Oliver Goldsmith

July 6

"If you're going to do something tonight that you'll be sorry for tomorrow morning, sleep late."

– Henny Youngman

July 7

"In wine there is wisdom, in beer there is Freedom, in water there is bacteria."

– Benjamin Franklin

July 8

"Corporation, n. An ingenious device for obtaining individual profit without individual responsibility."

– Ambrose Bierce

July 9

"The two most common elements in the universe are hydrogen and stupidity."

– Harlan Ellison

July 10

"Since I don't smoke, I decided to grow a mustache - it is better for the health."

– Salvador Dalí

July 11

"That woman speaks eighteen languages, and can't say 'No' in any of them."

— Dorothy Parker

July 12

"If a man could have half of his wishes, he would double his troubles."

— Benjamin Franklin

July 13

"Leave something for someone but dont leave someone for something."

— Enid Blyton

July 14

"A banker is a fellow who lends you his umbrella when the sun is shining, but wants it back the minute it begins to rain."

— Mark Twain

July 15

"Reader, suppose you were an idiot. And suppose you were a member of Congress. But I repeat myself."

— Mark Twain

July 16

"Gravitation is not responsible for people falling in love."

— Albert Einstein

July 17

"As you get older three things happen. The first is your memory goes, and I can't remember the other two."

— Norman Wisdom

July 18

"We are all born ignorant, but one must work hard to remain stupid."

—Benjamin Franklin

July 19

"Writing in English is the most ingenious torture ever devised for sins committed in previous lives. The English reading public explains the reason why."

— James Joyce

July 20

"Marriage is the chief cause of divorce."

— Groucho Marx

July 21

"A lie gets halfway around the world before the truth has a chance to get its pants on."

– Winston Churchill

July 22

"The older I grow, the more I distrust the familiar doctrine that age brings wisdom."

– H.L. Mencken

July 23

"That would be a good thing for them to cut on my tombstone: Wherever she went, including here, it was against her better judgment."

– Dorothy Parker

July 24

"Common sense and a sense of humor are the same thing, moving at different speeds. A sense of humor is just common sense, dancing."

– William James

July 25

"I am only human, although I regret it."

– Mark Twain

July 26

"The first time I sang in the church choir; two hundred people changed their religion."

– Fred Allen

July 27

"If life was fair, Elvis would be alive and all the impersonators would be dead."

– Johnny Carson

July 28

"If you find it hard to laugh at yourself, I would be happy to do it for you."

– Groucho Marx

July 29

"If any of you cry at my funeral I'll never speak to you again."

– Stan Laurel

July 30

"Writing is the only profession where no one considers you ridiculous if you earn no money."

– Jules Renard

July 31

"The avoidance of taxes is the only intellectual pursuit that still carries any reward."

– John Maynard Keynes

August

August 1

"I am an old man and have known a great many troubles, but most of them never happened."

– Mark Twain

August 2

"I believe in luck: how else can you explain the success of those you don't like?"

– Jean Cocteau

August 3

"A judge is a law student who marks his own examination papers."

– H. L. Mencken

August 4

"Writing a book is an adventure. To begin with, it is a toy and an amusement. Then it becomes a mistress, then it becomes a master, then it becomes a tyrant. The last phase is that just as you are about to be reconciled to your servitude, you kill the monster and fling him to the public."

— Winston S. Churchill

August 5

"Student: Dr. Einstein, Aren't these the same questions as last year's final exam?

Dr. Einstein: Yes; But this year the answers are different."

— Albert Einstein

August 6

"It's true hard work never killed anybody, but I figure, why take the chance?"

— Ronald Reagan

August 7

"Invisible things are the only realities."

— Edgar Allan Poe, Loss of Breath

August 8

"I don't believe in astrology; I'm a Sagittarius and we're skeptical."

— Arthur C. Clarke

August 9

"I require three things in a man: he must be handsome, ruthless, and stupid."

— Dorothy Parker

August 10

"I don't know much about being a millionaire, but I'll bet I'd be darling at it."

— Dorothy Parker

August 11

"Forgive your enemies, but never forget their names."

— John F. Kennedy

August 12

"I have noticed that the people who are late are often so much jollier than the people who have to wait for them."

— E. V. Lucas

August 13

"Speak when you are angry and you will make the best speech you will ever regret."

— Ambrose Bierce

August 14

"What the world needs is more geniuses with humility; there are so few of us left."

— Oscar Levant

August 15

"Have no fear of perfection. You'll never reach it."

– Salvador Dali

August 16

"Substitute 'damn' every time you're inclined to write 'very;' your editor will delete it and the writing will be just as it should be."

– Mark Twain

August 17

"Worrying is like paying a debt you don't owe."

– Mark Twain

August 18

"I like work: it fascinates me. I can sit and look at it for hours."

– Jerome K. Jerome

August 19

"An alcoholic is someone you don't like who drinks as much as you do."

– Dylan Thomas

August 20

"You want a friend in this city? [Washington, DC.] Get a dog!"

— Harry S. Truman

August 21

"He may look like an idiot and talk like an idiot but don't let that fool you. He really is an idiot."

— Groucho Marx

August 22

"Clothes make the man. Naked people have little or no influence on society."

— Mark Twain

August 23

"The Lord prefers common-looking people. That is why he made so many of them."

— Abraham Lincoln

August 24

"Every morning when I wake up, I experience an exquisite joy —the joy of being Salvador Dalí— and I ask myself in rapture: What wonderful things is this Salvador Dalí going to accomplish today?"

— Salvador Dalí

August 25

"He who laughs last didn't get the joke."

– Charles de Gaulle

August 26

"The only time a woman really succeeds in changing a man is when he is a baby."

– Natalie Wood

August 27

"My formula for success is rise early, work late, and strike oil."

J. P. Getty

August 28

"Patriotism is your conviction that this country is superior to all others because you were born in it."

– George Bernard Shaw

August 29

"Even on the most solemn occasions I got away without wearing socks and hid that lack of civilization in high boots"

– Albert Einstein

August 30

"A pessimist is a person who has had to listen to too many optimists."

– Don Marquis

August 31

"People say nothing is impossible, but I do nothing every day."

– A. A. Milne

September

September 1

"I don't want any yes-men around me. I want everybody to tell me the truth even if it costs them their job."

– Samuel Goldwyn

September 2

"The reports of my death are greatly exaggerated."

– Mark Twain

September 3

"I am free of all prejudice. I hate everyone equally. "

– W.C. Fields

September 4

"I was married by a judge. I should have asked for a jury."

– Groucho Marx

September 5

"If you think nobody cares if you're alive, try missing a couple of car payments."

– Earl Wilson

September 6

The weather is like the government, always in the wrong.

– Jerome K. Jerome

September 7

"It is not necessary for the public to know whether I am joking or whether I am serious, just as it is not necessary for me to know it myself."

– Salvador Dali

September 8

"All the things I really like to do are either immoral, illegal or fattening."

– Alexander Woollcott

September 9

"There are things that are so serious that you can only joke about them."

– Werner Heisenberg

September 10

"My own business always bores me to death; I prefer other people's."

— Oscar Wilde

September 11

"If evolution really works, how come mothers only have two hands?"

— Milton Berle

September 12

"It is hard enough to remember my opinions, without also remembering my reasons for them!"

— Friedrich Nietzsche

September 13

"I was gratified to be able to answer promptly, and I did. I said I didn't know."

— Mark Twain

September 14

"You see, wire telegraph is a kind of a very, very long cat. You pull his tail in New York and his head is meowing in Los Angeles. Do you understand this? And radio operates exactly the same way: you send signals here, they receive them there. The only difference is that there is no cat."

— Albert Einstein

September 15

"I drink to make other people more interesting."

— Ernest Hemingway

September 16

"If you can't convince them, confuse them."

— Harry S. Truman

September 17

"A great pleasure in life is doing what people say you cannot do."

— Walter Bagehot

September 18

"Everything is funny as long as it is happening to somebody else."

— Will Rogers

September 19

"I can't understand why a person will take a year to write a novel when he can easily buy one for a few dollars."

– Fred Allen

September 20

"Everybody's got to believe in something. I believe I'll have another beer."

– W.C. Fields

September 21

"Stupid men are the only ones worth knowing after all."

– Jane Austen

September 22

"An idealist is one who, on noticing that a rose smells better than a cabbage, concludes that it makes a better soup."

– H.L. Mencken, A Book of Burlesques

September 23

"The play was a great success, but the audience was a dismal failure."

– George Bernard Shaw

September 24

"I dream of a better tomorrow, where chickens can cross the road and not be questioned about their motives."

– Ralph Waldo Emerson

September 25

"Women are meant to be loved, not to be understood."

– Oscar Wilde

September 26

"My doctor told me that jogging could add years to my life. I think he was right. I feel ten years older already."

– Milton Berle

September 27

"Man cannot live by bread alone; he must have peanut butter."

James A. Garfield

September 28

"The average dog is a nicer person than the average person."

– Andy Rooney

September 29

"A clear conscience is the sure sign of a bad memory."

– Mark Twain

September 30

"My grandfather once told me that there were two kinds of people: those who do the work and those who take the credit. He told me to try to be in the first group; there was much less competition."

– Indira Gandhi

Funny Story 4

When Albert Einstein was working in Princeton university, one day he was going back home he forgot his home address.

The driver of the cab did not recognize him.

Einstein asked the driver if he knows Einstein's home.

The driver said "Who does not know Einstein's address?

Everyone in Princeton knows.

Do you want to meet him?".

Einstein replied "I am Einstein.

I forgot my home address, can you take me there? "

The driver reached him to his home and did not even collect his fare from him .

October

October 1

"All men are equal before fish."

– Herbert Hoover

October 2

"A pessimist is a man who thinks everybody is as nasty as himself, and hates them for it."

– George Bernard Shaw

October 3

"I would have written a shorter letter, but I did not have the time."

– Mark Twain

October 4

"I prefer someone who burns the flag and then wraps themselves up in the Constitution over someone who burns the Constitution and then wraps themselves up in the flag."

– Molly Ivins

October 5

"A rich man is nothing but a poor man with money."

– W. C. Fields

October 6

"Every man has his follies—and often they are the most interesting thing he has got."

Josh Billings

October 7

"The safe way to double your money is to fold it over once and put it in your pocket."

– Kin Hubbard

October 8

"Don't keep a man guessing too long – he's sure to find the answer somewhere else."

– Mae West

October 9

"I hate women because they always know where things are."

– Voltaire

October 10

"I could tell that my parents hated me. My bath toys were a toaster and a radio."

— Rodney Dangerfield

October 11

"I never made one of my discoveries through the process of rational thinking"

— Albert Einstein

October 12

"My doctor gave me six months to live, but when I couldn't pay the bill he gave me six months more."

— Walter Matthau

October 13

"Two things are infinite: the universe and human stupidity; and I'm not sure about the universe."

— Albert Einstein

October 14

"The only reason some people get lost in thought is because it's unfamiliar territory."

— Paul Fix

October 15

"Life is a sexually transmitted disease."

– R. D. Laing

October 16

"There's a fine line between genius and insanity. I have erased this line."

– Oscar Levant

October 17

"Have you noticed that all the people in favor of birth control are already born?"

– Benny Hill

October 18

"Egotist, n. A person of low taste, more interested in himself than in me."

– Ambrose Bierce,

October 19

"Going to church doesn't make you a Christian any more than going to a garage makes you an automobile."

– Billy Sunday

October 20

"Better die an old maid, sister, than marry the wrong man."

— Billy Sunday

October 21

"War is God's way of teaching Americans geography."

— Ambrose Bierce

October 22

"I am not strange. I am just not normal."

— Salvador Dalí

October 23

"I don't do drugs. I am drugs."

— Salvador Dali

October 24

"Always forgive your enemies – nothing annoys them so much."

— Oscar Wilde

October 25

"Laughing at our mistakes can lengthen our own life. Laughing at someone else's can shorten it."

– Cullen Hightower

October 26

"True terror is to wake up one morning and discover that your high school class is running the country."

– Kurt Vonnegut

October 27

"If I want to knock a story off the front page, I just change my hairstyle."

– Hillary Clinton

October 28

"The greatest thief this world has ever produced is procrastination, and he is still at large."

– Josh Billings

October 29

"Children today are tyrants. They contradict their parents, gobble their food, and tyrannize their teachers."

– Socrates

October 30

"Always remember that you are absolutely unique. Just like everyone else."

– Margaret Mead

October 31

"Whoever said money can't buy happiness didn't know where to shop."

– Gertrude Stein

November

November 1

"I don't make jokes. I just watch the government and report the facts."

— Will Rogers

November 2

"Before marriage, a man declares that he would lay down his life to serve you; after marriage, he won't even lay down his newspaper to talk to you."

— Helen Rowland

November 3

The person, be it gentleman or lady, who has not pleasure in a good novel, must be intolerably stupid."

— Jane Austen

November 4

"I didn't have time to write a short letter, so I wrote a long one instead."

— Mark Twain

November 5

"Always borrow money from a pessimist. He won't expect it back."

– Oscar Wilde

November 6

"The difference between stupidity and genius is that genius has its limits."

– Albert Einstein

November 7

"The only way to keep your health is to eat what you don't want, drink what you don't like, and do what you'd rather not."

– Mark Twain

November 8

"A Penny Saved is a Penny Earned"

– Benjamin Franklin

November 9

"Why is there so much month left at the end of the money?"

– John Barrymore

November 10

"I didn't fail the test, I just found 100 ways to do it wrong."

– Benjamin Franklin

November 11

"God is at home, it's we who have gone out for a walk."

– Meister Eckhart

November 12

"It's a recession when your neighbor loses his job; it's a depression when you lose yours."

– Harry S. Truman

November 13

"A black cat crossing your path signifies that the animal is going somewhere."

– Groucho Marx

November 14

"Cleaning up with children around is like shoveling during a blizzard."

– Margaret Culkin Banning

November 15

"No man has a good enough memory to be a successful liar."

Abraham Lincoln

November 16

"I was sorry to have my name mentioned as one of the great authors, because they have a sad habit of dying off. Chaucer is dead, Spencer is dead, so is Milton, so is Shakespeare, and I'm not feeling so well myself."

— Mark Twain

November 17

"I don't care what is written about me so long as it isn't true."

— Dorothy Parker

November 18

"I see no advantage in these new clocks. They run no faster than the ones made 100 years ago."

— Henry Ford

November 19

"No matter how much the cats fight, there always seem to be plenty of kittens. "

— Abraham Lincoln

November 20

I guess I don't so much mind being old, as I mind being fat and old.

Benjamin Franklin

November 21

The problem with socialism is that you eventually run out of other peoples' money.

Margaret Thatcher

November 22

"If at first you don't succeed, try, try again. Then quit. There's no point in being a damn fool about it."

– W. C. Fields

November 23

 "The only thing that stops God from sending another flood is that the first one was useless."

– Nicolas Chamfort

November 24

"I refuse to join any club that would have me as a member."

– Groucho Marx

November 25

"The secret of the demagogue is to make himself as stupid as his audience so they believe they are clever as he."

– Karl Kraus

November 26

"Guests, like fish, begin to smell after three days."

– Benjamin Franklin

November 27

"An American monkey, after getting drunk on brandy, would never touch it again, and thus is much wiser than most men."

– Charles Darwin

November 28

"Some people never go crazy. What truly horrible lives they must lead."

– Charles Bukowski

November 29

"I came from a real tough neighborhood. Once a guy pulled a knife on me. I knew he wasn't a professional, the knife had butter on it."

– Rodney Dangerfield

November 30

"Decision making, like coffee, needs a cooling process."

— George Washington

December

December 1

"What a kid I got, I told him about the birds and the bees and he told me about the butcher and my wife."

— Rodney Dangerfield

December 2

"Behind every successful man stands a surprised mother-in-law."

— Voltaire

December 3

"I am so clever that sometimes I don't understand a single word of what I am saying."

— Oscar Wilde

December 4

"Opportunity is missed by most people because it is dressed in overalls and looks like work."

— Thomas A. Edison

December 5

"Every man is guilty of all the good he did not do."

– Voltaire

December 6

"It is amazing what you can accomplish if you do not care who gets the credit."

— Harry S. Truman

December 7

"If I were two-faced, would I be wearing this one?"

— Abraham Lincoln

December 8

"It is a very funny thing that the sleepier you are, the longer you take about getting to bed."

— C.S. Lewis

December 9

"He that is good for making excuses is seldom good for anything else."

— Benjamin Franklin

December 10

"You live but once; you might as well be amusing."

— Coco Chanel

December 11

"Never go to a doctor whose office plants have died."

— Erma Bombeck

December 12

"A woman is like a tea bag – you can't tell how strong she is until you put her in hot water."

— Eleanor Roosevelt

December 13

"What is important is to spread confusion, not eliminate it."

— Salvador Dalí

December 14

"You have enemies? Good. That means you've stood up for something, sometime in your life."

— Winston Churchill

December 15

Never argue with stupid people, they will drag you down to their level and then beat you with experience.

— Mark Twain

December 16

"It is not enough to conquer; one must learn to seduce."

— Voltaire

December 17

"I believe in intuitions and inspirations...I sometimes FEEL that I am right. I do not KNOW that I am."

— Albert Einstein

December 18

"Always remember, that I have taken more out of alcohol than alcohol has taken out of me."

— Winston S. Churchill

December 19

"I know now that what makes a fool is an inability to take even his own good advice."

December 20

"An idea that is not dangerous is unworthy of being called an idea at all."

— Oscar Wilde

December 21

"If you find it hard to laugh at yourself, I would be happy to do it for you."

— Groucho Marx

December 22

"Money may not buy happiness, but I'd rather cry in a Jaguar than on a bus."

— Françoise Sagan

December 23

Democracy is a pathetic belief in the collective wisdom of individual ignorance.

— H.L. Mencken

December 24

"The day shit is worth money, poor people will be born without an asshole"

— Gabriel García Márquez,

December 25

"When a stupid man is doing something he is ashamed of, he always declares that it is his duty."

— George Bernard Shaw

December 26

"In order to acquire a growing and lasting respect in society, it is a good thing, if you possess great talent, to give, early in your youth, a very hard kick to the right shin of the society that you love. After that, be a snob."

— Salvador Dalí

December 27

"I hate writing, but I love having written."

— Dorothy Parker

December 28

"When you get a thing the way you want it, leave it alone."

— Winston S. Churchill

December 29

"It is easier to make money from money than it is to make money from business. Don't take the acumen of bankers as any guide for business, all they know is money."

— Henry Ford

December 30

"When we first got married, we made a pact. It was this: In our life together, it was decided I would make all of the big decisions and my wife would make all of the little decisions. For fifty years, we have held true to that agreement. I believe that is the reason for the success in our marriage. However, the strange thing is that in fifty years, there hasn't been one big decision."

— Albert Einstein

December 31

"I do not fear death. I had been dead for billions and billions of years before I was born, and had not suffered the slightest inconvenience from it."

— Mark Twain

Dear reader.

A good rating and your positive review are incredibly important for us!

If you have any comments or suggestion, please visit our website and let us know.

Thank you,

brain-words.com

"The noblest art is that of making others happy"

— P.T. Barnum

www.ingramcontent.com/pod-product-compliance
Lightning Source LLC
Chambersburg PA
CBHW020325290526
45785CB00007B/2922